ANDY & JANINE MASON

Dream
JOURNEY
WORKBOOK

Practical Steps to Pursuing Your Dreams
© 2012. Andy and Janine Mason
All rights reserved.

Cover design, book design and formatting by Lorraine Box: Propheticart@sbcglobal.net
Edited by Robert and Mary Sutherland, Redding, California, USA.
Author's Photo by Firefly Mobile Studio: www.firefly2u.com

ISBN-13: 978-1469965369
ISBN-10: 1469965364

*To order more resources or to learn more about the authors,
you may visit their website:*

www.iDreamCulture.com

Dream
JOURNEY
CONTENTS

Welcome to your

Dream JOURNEY

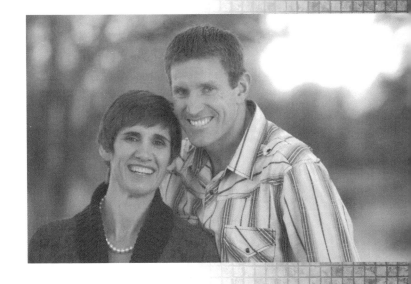

This workbook was developed by the Dream Culture team to give you practical step-by-step tools to pursue your dreams.

Our dream is to inspire and empower you to join us as we catalyze an entire culture of Dreamers. A Dream Culture is a community of people so bonded together by powerful relationships that the impossible is transformed into a logical expectation. It's where people encourage and empower each other to discover their destiny and live out their dreams. It's a culture overflowing with courage to face the impossible, where love overcomes fear and the tangible presence and power of God makes the supernatural a daily experience. It's a culture where people genuinely know each other and are committed to helping one another discover the rich treasure of gifts, talents and abilities God has placed in each one of us, and where we walk alongside one other to see the fullness of that treasure expressed.

As we work with people of all ages, experience and interests, our greatest reward is seeing their lives transformed and become who they were born to be. We have had the privilege of partnering with people and sharing the joy of their victory celebrated as they overcome dream barriers and experience dreams become reality. When people begin to shine and new life is released in them, we

are again reminded that we really are made in the image of God.

What Saint Irenaeus was quoted to have said in 202 AD still holds true today, *"the glory of God is a man fully alive."* Since Christ came that we might experience life that is abundant and full, then discovering and living your dreams is life with abundance. All creation is groaning in anticipation of seeing you and the people around you become *fully alive!*

Start living fully alive by discovering who you are as a son or daughter of God. Next, embrace the reality of what your true identity looks like as you connect with the dreams and desires God planted in your heart from before time began.

Together we get to walk out those dreams, one step at a time. Then we get to inspire and encourage the people around us to do the same.

Grace on your Dream Journey...

Andy & Janine Mason

Dream JOURNEY

Ready, Set... *Go!*

Going After a Dream is Like Going on a Journey

Impossible is just a big word thrown around by small men who find it easier to live in the world they've been given than explore the power they have to change it. Impossible is not a fact. It's an opinion. Impossible is not a declaration. It's a dare. Impossible is potential. Impossible is temporary. Impossible is nothing.

Adidas

TESTIMONIES *"Do it again!"*

Leader Freed from Depression: A leader had been fighting depression for five years. As he started the Dream Journey his depression left and within 12 months he had seen over 40 of his dreams realized, some of them dating back more than 20 years.

Big Game Fishing: One man wrote to go big game fishing on his Dream List. Just two weeks later the people he would be meeting on a future speaking engagement

1

contacted him. They asked, *"I know you were planning to leave on the Monday after the event, but we were wondering if you would like to delay your return flight because we have the best big game fishing in the world and we would like to take you fishing on that Monday?"*

Learning Spanish: Another man had a dream to learn Spanish. Within a few weeks of writing this dream down his landlord approached him and offered him a Rosetta Stone Spanish learning kit saying, *"I ordered this but they sent me the wrong one and now they won't take it back. Do you want it?"*

We have seen people purchase houses, start businesses and take their marriages to a whole new level. Others have given themselves permission to pursue painting, writing, dancing and performing and are now living a new abundant life.

As one dreamer said when she started the Dream Journey and saw how God moved on her behalf, *"I guess He just loves me!"*

WHAT IS A DREAM?

A dream is a picture of the future that I want to live in some day. Dreams are hope carriers and are not bound by time or reality.

"Dreams are seeds of possibility planted in your soul, calling you to pursue a unique path to the realization of your purpose."

John Maxwell

"Dreams are powerful. Dreams and those who live them can change cultures, redirect nations and move mountains."

Tony Stoltzfus

"God had a dream and wrapped your body around it."

Lou Engle

DREAM ACTIVATION EXERCISE: Remember a Dream

Choose a dream that you have already accomplished. Maybe you made the basketball team or reached the finals in a speech competition. Maybe it was getting married, having children or getting a promotion at work. Choose one dream and let your thoughts go back to the details of fulfilling that dream. Allow yourself to relive the emotions of that moment. What did it feel like when all the hard work you put in finally paid off and you fulfilled that dream? What emotions were released inside of you as you realized your dream? What did it look like, feel like, sound like, taste like and smell like?

How did you feel when you accomplished one of your dreams?

....

....

....

....

Now go back to that same dream and think about who was around you when it became a reality? How did it affect them? What impact did it have in their lives?

What happened in others as you accomplished your dream?

....

....

....

....

WHY BE A DREAMER?

*Hope deferred makes the heart sick, but a desire fulfilled is **a tree of life**.*

Proverbs 13:12

- **Life is released all around you.**

   Life is released all around you when you accomplish your dream.

   When you live out the things that God has placed in your heart, life is released around

you for all to see. It is a beautiful thing to see people doing what they were born to do. It draws people and inspires them to live their dreams also.

So what were you made for? What are the things in your heart?

- **All Creation is waiting for YOU**

  The revelation of the sons of God is you, fully alive, fully living what you were made to do, discovering your purpose and going after it.

  God's heart is that you discover His design for you, that you become all He made you to be and that you live it well. Then the glory of God can be released through you to the people around you.

  For I consider that the suferings of this present time are not worthy to be compared with the glory which shall be revealed in us. For the earnest expectation of the creation eagerly waits for the revealing of the sons of God.

  Romans 8:18-19

- **You have a divine mandate to dream**

  God made each and every person with the potential to positively affect the world. Your gifts, skills, passion and personality all combine to uniquely equip you to impact the world around you in a way that no other person can.

  You have a divine mandate to dream because when you embrace who you were created to be, it is impossible for the world around you not to be impacted in a significant way.

  All of Heaven is pulling for you to live your dreams so that you will impact the world as God has planned.

- **We must dream bigger in order to see global transformation**

  Global transformation is entirely possible when we each accept that living out our God-given dream is the key to affecting our community, our city, our nation and every other nation.

  The earth is waiting for us to reveal who God really is by demonstrating His glory. That revelation comes as each of us encounters God, discovers who we are and then walks into the fullness of our life in Him. When we walk in that fullness, we will impact every realm of society by demonstrating who God is.

- **Heaven is waiting**

  The cloud of witnesses mentioned in Hebrews 12:1 is cheering each of us on to live out our dreams and become all that we are called to be. They have gone before us and their lives are examples of the goodness of God. They left us a heritage of courage, hope and faith that echoes from ages past and into eternity.

But even more, God wants to release resources to you to live your dreams. He is waiting for you to make a commitment to go after your dreams. We continue to be amazed at the divine connections, release of resources and supernatural happenings that take place when someone simply puts their dreams onto paper and makes a conscious decision to go after them.

Is it possible that angels are waiting to be released to act on our behalf? What if we believed in ourselves as much as our Heavenly Father believes in us? What if we embraced what Jesus said in Matthew 18:19? "Again I say to you that if two of you agree on earth concerning anything that they ask, it will be done for them by My Father in Heaven."

> *Write the vision and make it plain on tablets, that he may run who reads it.*
>
> **Habakkuk 2:2**

YOU HAVE PERMISSION TO DREAM

Father God gives you permission to dream. He is for your dreams and wants you to live them out.

DREAM ACTIVATION EXERCISE: Permission to Dream

How does knowing that God is for your dreams change the way you think about dreams?

....

....

....

....

Dream Time:

Writing a Dream List is powerful because it takes the things that are in your heart and puts them in a more tangible way on paper. How you record your dreams is up to you. The goal is to have them recorded in a way that makes them accessible to you to review them regularly and continually inspire you to go after them.

Some people like to create a Dream Board with inspiring pictures, or use a Dream Journal or Dream Cache to record their journey.

You will notice that we have left a number of pages (some lined, some blank) for you to record your dreams. Don't be intimidated. Going after your dreams is a journey and an on-going process. Once you have started to check off some of your dreams you will want to add to the list.

You will have some time in your Dream Journey Class to begin your list but you will want to add to your list outside of the class time. Below are some tips to help you on your way:

- **Find the place that works best for you to be creative.** It may be that you are inspired by a quiet place by a stream, or it may be the energy of your favorite coffee shop that gets your creative juices flowing. Find the time and space that works for you.

- **Connect with the Father.** Your Heavenly Father designed you to dream and wants to help reawaken and increase that ability. When you are seated in Heavenly places you are not limited by the restrictions you feel are imposed on you by your circumstances. This is the place to dream. Ask God to show you how He sees you, then dream from that place.

- **Set your mind on things above.** Consciously choose to set your mind to operate from Heaven's perspective where nothing is impossible! At this point, don't think about how you will achieve your dream or you will likely discount things that seem out of reach. Keep at the forefront of your mind that things that now seem impossible may later be achieved. Write down all the dreams that come to mind and sift them later. Remember it is your list so you can change or amend it at any time.

- **Ask yourself questions.**

    How would I live if I were fearless?

    If money were no object, what would I do?

    How would I live if I believed...?

    Who do I want to be?

    What things do I want to do?

    What things do I want to have?

- **Consider the above questions in these different categories:** *physical, financial, emotional, spiritual and legacy dreams*

- **How would I live if I believed that nothing was impossible?**

(Further questions to help you discover your dreams are offered at the back of this workbook)

- **Some examples of dreams to get you started**

Big Dreams	End global poverty; become the first woman president...
Fun Dreams	Ride in a hot air balloon; eat a whole tub of ice cream...
Physical Dreams	Run a marathon; beat an illness; go skydiving...
Financial Dreams	Become debt free; give away a house...
Emotional Dreams	Overcome fear; restore a broken relationship...
Spiritual Dreams	Live from love; be known as a friend of God...
Legacy Dreams	Pass on an inheritance to my children's children...

MY DREAM LIST

Start entering your dreams below in whatever order they come to you. Consider the following categories:

Things To _BE_   Things To _DO_   Things To _HAVE_

Now, within each of the above categories, consider different aspects of your life and the lives of people around you:

Physical   Financial   Emotional   Spiritual   Legacy

1. ....
2. ....
3. ....
4. ....
5. ....
6. ....
7. ....
8. ....
9. ....
10. ....
11. ....
12. ....
13. ....
14. ....
15. ....
16. ....
17. ....
18. ....

19. ....

20. ....

21. ....

22. ....

23. ....

24. ....

25. ....

26. ....

27. ....

28. ....

29. ....

30. ....

31. ....

32. ....

33. ....

34. ....

35. ....

36. ....

37. ....

38. ....

39. ....

40. ....

41. ....

42. ....

43. ....

44. ....

45. ....

46. ....

47. ....

48. ....

49. ....

50. ....

51. ....

52. ....

53. ....

54. ....

55. ....

56. ....

57. ....

58. ....

59. ....

60. ....

61. ....

62. ....

63. ....

64. ....

65. ....

66. ....

67. ....

68. ....

69. ....

70. ....

71. ....

72. ....

73. ....

74. ....

75. ....

76. ....

77. ....

78. ....

79. ....

80. ....

81. ....

82. ....

83. ....

84. ....

85. ....

86. ....

87. ....

88. ....

89. ....

90. ....

91. ....

92. ....

93. ....

94. ....

95. ....

96. ....

97. ....

98. ....

99. ....

100. ....

101. ....

102. ....

103. ....

104. ....

105. ....

106. ....

107. ....

108. ....

109. ....

110. ....

111. ....

112. ....

113. ....

114. ....

115. ....

116. ....

117. ....

118. ....

119. ....

120. ....

121. ....

122. ....

123. ....

124. ....

125. ....

126. ....

127. ....

128. ....

129. ....

130. ....

131. ....

132. ....

133. ....

134. ....

135. ....

136. ....

137. ....

138. ....

139. ....

140. ....

141. ....

142. ....

143. ....

144. ....

145. ....

146. ....

147. ....

148. ....

149. ....

150. ....

Dream JOURNEY

Building Momentum

Every Dream Journey Gains Momentum by Taking Simple Action Steps

SETTING YOU UP TO SUCCEED ON YOUR DREAM JOURNEY

- **Daily dream thoughts**

  Thinking about your dreams regularly keeps you positioned to recognize opportunities when they come your way. You naturally move toward whatever you stay focused on.

- **Daily dream goals**

  Progress is made by regularly taking small steps toward your dreams.

  "What am I doing today to move toward my dream?"

Dream
JOURNEY

- **Dream Friend or Partner** – *One who encourages you*

  You were not designed to pursue your dreams in isolation. You were meant to pursue your dreams within the environment of a community. Look for someone who will partner with you, one who has a heart to hear your heart and walk with you. Look for a person of faith who will join with you and believe that nothing is impossible.

"Keep away from people who try to belittle your ambition. Small people always do that. But the really great make you feel that you, too, can become great."

Mark Twain

PUTTING LEGS ON YOUR DREAMS

- **What dream do I pursue first?**

  Ask the Holy Spirit what dream to go after first. He knows your immediate circumstances and what is soon to come your way. What dream do you feel motivated to go after right now? When you think about it, which dream has life on it now? What dream are you working on now? What dream is currently surrounded by some beneficial circumstance that would increase the momentum for you to go after it right now?

DREAM ACTIVATION EXERCISE: The dream I want to start with now

- **Defining the Dream – turning it into a S.M.A.R.T. Goal**

Converting your dream into a specific goal brings more focus. The greater the focus you have, the more power you have to move forward. A dream can drift along outside the realities of time and resources, but a defined goal brings the clarity to move forward in a purposeful, structured way.

Sᴘᴇᴄɪꜰɪᴄ – *How clear is your dream?*

Mᴇᴀsᴜʀᴀʙʟᴇ – *How will you identify your progress toward your dream?*

Aᴛᴛᴀɪɴᴀʙʟᴇ – *Is your dream within your capabilities?*

Rᴇʟᴇᴠᴀɴᴛ - *How significant is this dream to you?*

Tɪᴍᴇ ʙᴀsᴇᴅ – *When will you start or complete your dream?*

DREAM ACTIVATION EXERCISE: From dream to S.M.A.R.T. goal

Now take the dream you have chosen to start with and put it through the S.M.A.R.T. goal process. Go through each category and add definition and clarity. Following are some questions to help you. *Used by permission, Tony Soltzfus, Coaching Questions*

SPECIFIC : You can state clearly where you are going.

⇒ *What will this dream look like when accomplished?*

⇒ *What has to be done to achieve this dream?*

⇒ *What do you need to be in order to achieve this dream?*

⇒ *What else can you tell me about this dream in order to be more specific?*

⇒ *What will be different when you have accomplished this dream?*

⇒ *How could you define this dream more clearly or restate it in fewer words?*

....

....

....

....

MEASURABLE: You have included a way to measure progress.

⇒ *How can you create a quantitative measurement of forward progress for your dream so you will know when you have accomplished it?*

⇒ *How will you and others know you have achieved progress toward this goal?*

⇒ *How would you know when you have moved closer to your goal of being better at something (like being a better husband, father or dancer)?*

⇒ *How could you re-word your goal to make it more measurable?*

....

....

....

....

ATTAINABLE: It is within your capabilities and depends only on you.

⇒ *Does this goal depend on anyone else's choices?*

⇒ *Is this goal within your capabilities?*

⇒ *Are there any barriers or circumstances working against you achieving this goal?*

⇒ *How can you re-word your goal statement so it depends only on you?*

....

....

....

....

....

RELEVANT: You care enough about this goal to make it a priority.

⇒ *What makes this important to you?*

⇒ *What things are you prepared to put aside in order to make this goal happen?*

⇒ *On a scale of one to ten, how important is it to you that you reach this goal?*

⇒ *How would you feel if you did not achieve this goal?*

....

....

....

....

....

TIME-SPECIFIC: It has a deadline or target completion date.

⇒ *When will you reach this goal?*

⇒ *When will this be an established habit?*

⇒ *When will you start this?*

⇒ *What is your targeted completion date?*

....

....

....

....

....

Once you have developed a one-sentence statement of your goal, write it down. Your goal should clearly state the objective you want to reach by a particular date. This will keep you focused in the process of developing action steps, reviewing the outcomes and continuing the process as your dream materializes right before your eyes.

My S.M.A.R.T. Goal:

....

....

....

....

....

Now share your S.M.A.R.T. goal with a partner. Have them give you feedback on how clear it is. Refine it if necessary. The objective is to present it in a format that increases its clarity so you can begin to gain measurable forward momentum.

DREAM ACTIVATION EXERCISE: Turning the Goal into Action Steps

Action steps can be developed as you clarify your goal even further. This allows you to choose one or more specific action steps that you can act on over the next week.

In order to create action steps you will ask yourself, or have a friend ask you, a series of simple questions.

What *could* you do to move forward now? List as many possibilities as you can.

....

....

....

....

What else could you do to move forward? Go beyond what you know. Think outside the box and ask the Holy Spirit to help you come up with some new options. This is where working with a friend can be helpful as they ask you questions that make you think from a different perspective. If you were in someone else's shoes, what would you do? What have you or others done in similar situations in the past that have been effective?

....

....

....

....

What do you *want* to do? Look at the options that you listed and choose one you feel will work best for you. Which one stands out to you the most? Which one motivates you into action?

....

....

....

What *will* you do? And *when* will you do it? Make a commitment to do that action step and don't forget to include when you will do it.

My action step:

....

....

....

Hope brings life. But in order to attain victory, hope must be accompanied by action. The dream you have will remain only a dream unless you make a conscious decision to turn it into tangible steps that you can walk out.

Graveyards all around the world are full of buried dreams. You can choose to take the steps that will turn your dreams into a reality. The choice is yours.

"Well done is better than well said."

Benjamin Franklin

Dream JOURNEY

SESSION THREE

Overcoming Setbacks

Each Dream Comes With Challenges and Obstacles to Overcome Along the Way

How you respond to those obstacles will determine whether or not you carry on in your journey.

Some of the main obstacles to your Dream Journey may come in the form of disappointment, discouragement and disillusionment. Learning to overcome these obstacles will allow you to continue on your journey and reach your dream.

Dis as a prefix means the opposite of something (Collins Concise English Dictionary). *Dis*-appointment is the opposite of appointment, *dis*-couragement steals your courage and *dis*-illusionment takes the illumination or hope from you.

- **Overcoming disappointment –** "Who do you think you are?"

  Albert Einstein is credited with having said, "It's not that I'm so smart. It's just that I stay with problems longer." He knew how to *not* give into disappointment.

  Disappointment has two definitions (Collins Concise English Dictionary):

  1. To fail to meet the expectation of, and
  2. To remove from office

  Disappointment happens when our expectations are not met. This leads to heartache and if left unattended, this heartache can lead to being dis-appointed in our role or identity.

  Disappointment asks, "Who do you think *you* are?" It causes us to wonder if we really are appointed for such a time as this. It undermines our belief in who we are and what we are capable of doing.

  In order to stay motivated and move forward in pursuit of our dreams, we must stay connected with who God says we are.

  The remedy to disappointment is to remember who you REALLY are. You are significant, valuable and unique. That revelation comes from being in God's Presence and listening to what He says about you. Turn your eyes from your circumstances and what they would try to tell you and turn again to Him. Sit on His lap and hear His words as He reminds you of who you are.

- **Regaining Courage –** "Do you *really* think you can?"

  The definition of discouragement is to be deprived of the will to persist in doing something (Collins Concise English Dictionary).

  Discouragement tempts us to give up on the journey. It speaks to us in such a way as to try to steal our courage. Discouragement asks, "Do you *really* think you can?"

  The remedy to discouragement is to find new courage. In 1 Samuel 30:6, we read about David when he was faced with an incredibly discouraging situation; his city was burned, his family was stolen and his men wanted to kill him. But David strengthened or *encouraged* himself in the Lord. He knew how to lean into the Presence of God, feel His comfort, hear His voice and receive His courage to continue. In the same way we each must turn our attention to God so we

Only be strong and of good courage.

Joshua 1:18

Be of good courage, And He shall strengthen your heart, All you who hope in the LORD.

Psalm 31:24

Dream
JOURNEY

can receive His strength and courage for our journey. Courage comes when you know you have a powerful Daddy who is on your side. The God who created the Heavens and the earth is *WITH YOU*. If God is with you and for you, who can be against you? (see Romans 8:31)

Another source of courage can be found in the people around you. This is where being part of the right community becomes so important. Having people around you who can encourage you on your Dream Journey is invaluable. Each of us will experience times when we need to receive encouragement from others, but we also need to develop a lifestyle of encouraging ourselves in the Lord.

- **Restoring Hope** – "Where do you think *you're* going?"

    Disillusionment is defined as the state of having had naïve faith destroyed (Merriam Webster Online Dictionary).

    Disillusionment comes when our faith gets eroded and our eyes become more focused on the problem than on the promise, the goal and the prize. Disillusionment steals our hope and asks, "Where do you think *you're* going?" If we listen to disillusionment we lose sight of our dream and our goal.

    So how can you keep your eyes on the goal?

    There are a number of practical things we can do to help us keep the vision before us, but the first place to get our vision *re-illuminated* is in God's Presence. Have your sight flooded again with His light, to again understand how He sees you and your circumstances. The view from His Throne is quite different than from here in the midst of our trials. As we spend time with Him, the One who made us, He restores hope and gives us fresh perspective and vision of where we are going.

    Remind yourself of God's promises for your future and how He has guided you in the past.

- **Resurrecting Dead Dreams**

    Ezekiel 37 tells the story of a valley of dry bones. In the second verse we read that the bones were very dry, in other words, well beyond any natural hope of resurrection. Yet God saw that they could come to life again!

    God partnered with Ezekiel to raise the bones to life. He used Ezekiel's words to speak the bones and sinews back together. He commanded Ezekiel to declare life and breath back into the bodies and as he did, the bodies lived!

    Many of us have experienced the death of a dream. The memory of that death holds

us captive. It's like the dead bones of that old dream speak to us and remind us of what *didn't* happen. They taunt us and tell us not to dream again, that it is too risky or too painful.

It's time to silence the voice of those dead dreams and let the voice of the Dream Giver speak again.

You have the power to partner with God and declare life back into your dreams. Those dreams may look a little different than they did before they died, but yet they can live again.

*When God restores something, it is always **better** than before.*

Ministry time:

....

....

....

....

....

....

....

....

....

....

....

....

So I prophesied as I was commanded; and as I prophesied, there was a noise, and suddenly a rattling; and the bones came together, bone to bone. Indeed, as I looked, the sinews and the flesh came upon them, and the skin covered them over; but there was no breath in them. Also He said to me, "Prophesy to the breath, prophesy, son of man, and say to the breath, 'Thus says the Lord GOD: "Come from the four winds, O breath, and breathe on these slain, that they may live."'" So I prophesied as He commanded me, and breath came into them, and they lived, and stood upon their feet, an exceedingly great army.

Ezekiel 37: 7 -10

God, who gives life to the dead and calls those things which do not exist as though they did.

Romans 4:17

Dream
JOURNEY

DREAM ACTIVATION EXERCISE: My Plan to Live *UNSTOPPABLE*

What could you do to keep the truth about you and your dreams in front of you?

What plan do you have for the next time your dreams are challenged?

What tools can you arm yourself with so that you are set up to overcome?

Dream
JOURNEY

BONUS DREAM ACTIVATION EXERCISE: God's Dream For Me

Reflect

You dream because you were made in the image of the most audacious *Dreamer* there is – God. He dreamed the whole universe up, and it came to be. And before you were born, He dreamed of you.

What is God's dream for you? Take some time to meditate on these questions and ask the Holy Spirit what He wants to show you about God's dream for you.

- God sees the best you, the real you He created you to be. What do you look like to Him?
- What is the picture God has in His mind of who you were made to be?
- What is God's dream for His relationship with you? What does He long for and look forward to for you?
- When God pictures His dream for you, how does it make Him feel?

....

....

....

....

Reinforce

Do this Dream Activation with your Dream Friend or Dream Partner. Both of you share what you saw as God's dream for your life. As you listen to each other, tune in to what the Holy Spirit would add to that dream. What else is in God's heart for each of you? Take time to pray, prophecy and affirm each other.

....

....

....

....

Face the Voices of the Past

Become aware of the voices that discourage you from pursuing your dreams. These are the things that you hear when you are at a critical juncture in pursuit of your dreams. Instead of trying to ignore the voices:

- Pull them to the surface. Ask yourself, what am I really thinking?

- Examine your thoughts in the light of the truth. Is this the voice of truth or a lie speaking to me? If you are unsure ask the Holy Spirit to reveal His truth to you. What does Jesus have to say about this?

- Ask a faith-filled friend to help you see the truth about you and your dreams.

- Choose to believe what God says about you rather than what your past failures or disappointments try to tell you.

- Declare the truth over yourself. For example: God is good and He is for my dreams. He has placed dreams in me and He will release Heaven's resources to see them lived out.

If you have had a series of past disappointments then you will need to continue dislodging old lies with new truth until truth becomes the revelation of God's plan for your future.

Dream
JOURNEY

Overcoming Mindsets

What You Believe Determines How You Experience
Your Dream Journey.

THE POWER OF WHAT WE BELIEVE

The following graphic illustrates the Dream Journey process. By now on your Dream Journey, you will have some outcomes from the action steps that you implemented. You may have an outcome that has progressed you toward your dream. If so, great! Continue by making a new action step.

Set your mind on things above, not on things on the earth.

Colossians 3:2

It may be you have an outcome that has presented you with setbacks that are hindering your progress. Often when we are faced with a challenge or setback we immediately assume it is something external rather than examining and dealing with the internal beliefs that hinder us.

In this session we deal with internal barriers to our progress. Many of the perceived external barriers such as limitations

of time, resources or ideas, are actually internal barriers. What we truly believe to be true about God, ourselves, and what we have access to is often more of a barrier than the external circumstances.

DREAM ACTIVATION EXERCISE: The Power of What We Believe

The purpose of this exercise is to become aware of what you really believe to be true. In order to do this well you must be completely honest with yourself.

A particular statement will be presented to you. When you read or hear this, capture and then write down the thoughts or feelings that first come to your mind.

What you believe will determine whether you begin to think of creative solutions (how this *can* be done) or creative defenses (why this *cannot* be done). The same is true in your Dream Journey. What you believe determines whether or not you will succeed.

When we are faced with opposition or obstacles to progress, our internal thought processes reveal what we believe to be true.

Let's go back to the Dream Activation Exercise above. Now take a moment and align your thinking with Heaven. In Heaven there are no limits. There is no financial lack in Heaven – even the streets are made of gold! There is no sickness in Heaven. There is no fear in Heaven. With God nothing is impossible. As you think from Heaven's perspective what creative solutions can you come up with to continue moving toward the fulfillment of your dream?

Heaven's perspective:

....

....

....

....

....

....

....

....

....

....

"Impossible is nothing!"

Adidas

OVERCOMING MINDSETS THAT HINDER US

What is a mindset? A mindset is a habit of the mind established by continually thinking on something.

Having your mind set on something is not the problem. It's what your mind is set on that can become the problem. The challenge is to keep your mind set on the things of Heaven, and see things as your Heavenly Father sees them. It is only then that His resources can be released and you can truly live out the prayer of Jesus, "On earth as it is in Heaven" (Matthew 6:10).

Set your mind on things above, not on things on the earth.

Colossians 3:2

As we highlight some of the most common mindsets that can hinder your Dream Journey, we encourage you to ask the Holy Spirit to speak to you about any mindsets that are stopping you from making progress. It may be one of the mindsets we present here, or it may be a totally different one. Either way, He wants to reveal truth to you and set you free from any hindering mindsets.

- **Servant Mindset** *"Just tell me what to do"*

  Having a servant's *heart* is a good thing. Greatness only comes through serving others. You never become too important to pick up the trash or clean the bathroom. However, a servant *mindset* says, "I'm *only* a servant; I *only* do what I'm told to do." A servant mindset dis-empowers people from thinking for themselves and from learning to live as a son or daughter of God in partnership WITH Him. We are invited to co-labor with God!

  No longer do I call you servants, for a servant does not know what his master is doing; but I have called you friends, for all things that I heard from My Father I have made known to you.

  John 15:15

  Galatians 3:29 – 4:7 talks about the process of becoming mature as we walk with the Lord. It describes how we all begin our walk with God as servants learning a completely new way of living life through submission and obedience. But God's intent is that we grow up into full spiritual maturity and become His friends. God's friends no longer need to be told what to do every moment of the day. Because His friends have learned His ways and know His heart they can take initiative. As you learn obedience and yield your will to Him, He will ask you what is in *your* heart, and then He will encourage you to go after those things.

  Delight yourself in the LORD, and He shall give you the desires of your heart.

  Psalm 37:4

  Son, you are always with me, and all that I have is yours.

  Luke 15:31b

Dream
JOURNEY

See yourself as a son or daughter of God. You have His permission to discover the desires of your heart and go after them.

■ **Hamster Mindset** *"I'm too busy"*

The hamster mindset comes from a false belief that being busy for God is the same as being productive for God. Just like a hamster running on a wheel in its cage, we can run very fast but not make any forward progress. Genesis 3:17-19 tells us that striving is part of the curse that sin brought upon mankind. But Jesus came to break every curse.

Christ has redeemed us from the curse of the law, having become a curse for us.

Galatians 3:13a

Jesus came to bring us freedom. He invites us into a restored connection with the Father where we can live from a place of rest and cease our striving. It is a gift!

Everything we now do can come from a place of rest and peace, born from our connection with Him. When we live from His Presence we live from rest. No longer do we need to be so busy that we don't have time to do the things that are really on our hearts or pursue the dreams He has placed there. We must learn to protect our highest priorities to prevent busyness from stealing away things that are most important to us.

What does your life say about your priorities? When was the last time you stopped to review how you have spent your time and examined how productive that time has been? What is most important to you? You priorities will be revealed by what you give your time to.

Come to me, all you who labor and are heavy laden, and I will give you rest.

Matthew 11:28

The only person that has complete responsibility and authority over your time is you!

■ **Lottery Mindset** *"Someone will do it for me"*

Most of the time it takes many years and a lot of hard work to become an overnight success.

The lottery mindset says, "I can just pray and wait and something will happen on my behalf." Underneath the lottery mindset is the belief that, "I'm not responsible for

me." It's like a spiritual lottery where you direct your faith toward God but just sit back and wait for Him to move on your behalf. The truth is that we are in a partnership with God and we must co-labor with Him to see our dreams fulfilled. It takes faith *and* action to become the person God has made you to be.

As James shows us, *"Show me your faith without your works, and I will show you my faith by my works...faith without works is dead..."* (*see* James 2:18, 26). We show our faith by what we do, by putting action to our faith.

...faith without works is dead...

James 2:26

You are powerful! God will not do for you what you can do for yourself. A partnership requires action by both parties. If God did everything for you that wouldn't be a true partnership and, in fact, it would actually dis-empower you. God wants to teach you how to partner with Heaven. Start with what is in your hand now and watch Him make the impossible *suddenly* happen.

If I do not do the works of My Father, do not believe Me.

John 10:37

What has God already placed in your hand? What do you need to do today to walk toward your dream?

- **Grasshopper Mindset** *"I'm too small, too big, too young, too old..."*

The thirteenth chapter of Numbers tells the story of twelve leaders of Israel who were chosen and sent to spy out the Promised Land. All twelve spies reported how good the land was and how it "flowed with milk and honey." They all acknowledged the presence of the existing inhabitants of the land who would have to be defeated in order for Israel to take possession of the land. Two of the spies returned bursting with confidence, "We can do this." But ten out of the twelve came back saying, "We were like grasshoppers in our own sight, and so we were in their sight."

There we saw the giants; and we were like grasshoppers in our own sight, and so we were in their sight.

Numbers 13:33

Because these ten spies saw themselves as weak and small in comparison with the giants, they concluded that they would not be able to possess their Promised Land. They chose not to believe what God had promised them. They quit before the fight had even started.

Yet in all these things we are more than conquerors through Him who loved us.

Romans 8:37

The way they saw themselves prevented them from going after their dream.

Let's learn from their mistake. Philippians 4:13 says, *"I can do all things through Christ who strengthens me."* The obstacles

Dream
JOURNEY

you find in your way can become the very stepping-stones used to fulfill your dream.

"You miss 100% of the shots you don't take."

Wayne Gretzky

DREAM ACTIVATION EXERCISE: Encountering Truth

Being set free from mindsets that hold you in bondage requires that you see the truth. This comes through the revelation of who God is and who God says you are. Connect with him. Become aware of His Presence and then ask the following questions:

What mindset is hindering me from moving forward right now? It may be one of the four mindsets we described above or a different one that you became aware of during this session.

And you shall know the truth, and the truth shall make you free.

John 8:32

I am the way, the truth, and the life.

John 14:6a

. . . .

. . . .

. . . .

. . . .

What is the truth? Ask the Lord to show you the truth that can overpower any lie hidden within the mindset you are currently dealing with. For example, if you are dealing with the grasshopper mindset, ask God to show you how He sees you.

. . . .

. . . .

. . . .

. . . .

Dream
JOURNEY

Now, what will you do in response to what He said? What one thing will you do differently this week to build on your new Heavenly mindset?

....

....

....

....

....

BONUS DREAM ACTIVATION EXERCISE

What is Your Mind Set On?

As you experienced this session, what thoughts, feelings or revelation did you become aware of in yourself?

- What do those feelings tell you about what you believe?

- If you were on the outside observing the way you live, what mindsets would you see evidenced?

- What would you like to do about that?

....

....

....

....

....

The way to establish mindsets built on truth is to first connect with the Spirit of Truth.

Take some time to connect with the Father, meditating on the above Scripture. Then ask yourself the following questions:

- What does it look or feel like to be hidden with Christ in God?

- Who are the Father and the Son to me?

- Who am I to the Father and the Son? A servant? A friend? A beloved companion?

- What is the Holy Spirit saying to me about who I am and who I was made to be?

- Which nature or aspect of Heaven do I want to set my mind on?

- What aspect of the nature of Christ do I most admire and resonate with? What do I bring to the earth?

If then you were raised with Christ, seek those things which are above, where Christ is, sitting at the right hand of God. Set your mind on things above, not on things on the earth. For you died, and your life is hidden with Christ in God.

Colossians 3:1-3

Living As a Friend of God - The Antidote to a Servant Mindset

You are a powerful decision maker designed to co-create with Heaven.

- How can you establish a mindset of being a friend of God who has a serving heart rather than a servant waiting for the next instruction from God?

- What has God given you to display through your life on the earth?

- What do your dreams say about what your life message or life purpose may be? What is in your heart to do?

- What does your Father want to co-create on the earth with you?

- What has He been saying to you?

- Take a moment to reflect on what you are hearing God say and write it down. Now ask yourself what one thing you will do differently this week to move forward and live your dreams as God intended.

....

....

....

....

....

Protecting the Priorities – The Antidote to a Hamster Mindset

If you don't protect what is important to you, no one else will.

- What does your schedule say about what is important to you? What is revealed about your priorities based on your daily or weekly activities?

- If you asked a friend or workmate, what would they say is most important to you?

- How much time do you spend on activities where you come away thinking, "That was a waste of time"? What will you do about that?

....

....

....

....

....

Consider doing the following activities to develop a lifestyle of living intentionally and purposefully:

- First, make a list of the top five to ten roles or priorities in your life. Consider roles such as being a friend of God, a husband or wife, a parent, a friend, a son or daughter or a leader in an area specific to your life's calling.

Dream
JOURNEY

- How would you like to be known in each of these key roles?

- What would you like to have said at your funeral?

- Now that you have identified your key roles and what you want to be known for, design a one or two sentence statement that captures this. For example, Andy has a priority of being a great husband. His statement defining this priority looks like this: *"Janine will say of me, 'He is my devoted companion and greatest champion. He lives as Christ to me in loving me into fullness of life. Together we establish a heavenly model of what a godly couple in ministry and life look like.'"*

Now consider what you could do to make these written priorities become established realities in your life.

- What could you do to remind yourself daily or weekly about what is most important to you?

- Who could you share your priorities with to help you keep accountable to your plan?

- How could you build these priorities into your week's activities and schedule?

- How are you going to protect time in your schedule for the pursuit of your dreams?

Living Powerfully – The Antidote to a Lottery Mindset

Living powerfully is about taking responsibility for doing your part of fulfilling God's plan for your life. It is about focusing on what you *can* do, not on what you *cannot* do. In considering your dreams think about the following:

- What are the things that are already in your hand that you could do something about now?

- How could you prepare, position and propel yourself to be ready when the next door to your dream opens?

Overcoming Mindsets | session four

- If you imagined one of your friends giving you advice about your dream, where do you think he or she would suggest you should start?

- What can you do that you are not currently doing?

- Ask the Holy Spirit to open your eyes to see what He has already placed in your hand, what is already within your reach or is accessible through the relationships around you.

  See Matthew 14:15 - 21

- In this partnership of moving forward in your dreams, ask the Holy Spirit what He will do and what you need to do.

....

....

....

....

....

What You Believe Determines How You Experience Your Dream Journey | 77

Dream JOURNEY

Staying Motivated

Staying Motivated is the Key to Finishing Your Dream Journey

The passion behind your dream is a powerful motivating force that keeps you moving forward on your Dream Journey. In order to keep motivated in tough times, it is vital to stay connected to this passion.

There is a difference between the motivation or passion behind the dream (the *contents*) and the medium through which the dream is expressed or experienced (the *cup*). For example, if your dream is to take the gospel to unreached people groups (*contents*) there are many ways this dream could be expressed that have nothing to do with going to some remote village (*cup*). You might discover unreached people groups in your surrounding community and reach them through the Internet or other media. You could even start a business that meets their needs and opens their hearts to hear your message. If you confuse the contents with the cup you will limit the options through which you can fulfill your dream.

When we discover the passion behind our dream and stay connected to that passion it will be easier to stay motivated to continue moving forward.

> *"The greatest glory in living lies not in never falling, but in rising every time we fall."*
>
> Nelson Mandela

Dream
JOURNEY

COACHING DEMONSTRATION: Tapping the Passion Behind a Dream

As you observe this demonstration, pay close attention to how the passion behind the dream is uncovered. Listen for how the following questions are repeated:

- "What's behind that?"

- "Tell me more about that."

- "I heard you say... tell me more about that."

Also watch for the visual and verbal clues that communicate Jenn's passion. Watch for:

- Facial expressions that reveal the emotion behind her answers

- The rise of her energy level and tone of her voice

- Words or phrases she repeats

- Emotive words. For example I was *born* for..., I *hate* that..., I *love*...

Observations:

....

....

....

....

....

....

....

....

....

....

DREAM ACTIVATION EXERCISE: Tapping the Passion Behind a Dream

Find a Dream Partner to join you in this exercise. Ask them about a dream they have. Then, using the simple questions and emotional clues previously demonstrated, help them tap into the passion behind their dream. When you have finished exploring their dream, change roles and have them help you tap into the passion behind your dream.

- "What's behind that?"

- "Tell me more about that."

- "I heard you say... tell me more about that."

The motivating passion behind my dream is:

....

....

....

....

....

....

OTHER FACTORS AFFECTING MOTIVATION

- **Ownership** – *Is this really your dream?*

    You are the only one who is responsible for making your dreams come true. There will be people along the way who impart their faith and courage to you when yours needs a boost. There may be people who support you financially, provide other resources or connect you to others who can help get you where you need to go. But in the end, your dream is *your* dream and you have to really *own* it in order to bring it to pass.

    What can take you beyond the limitations of your personal comfort zone in the pursuit of your dream? It's *ownership*, the mindset that says, "This thing belongs to me and I am willing to pay for it!"

    Are you willing to pay the price for your dream? Are you ready to commit energy, time and resources to pursue it? If no one else joins or supports you, will you still pursue it?

Dream
JOURNEY

- **Season** – *Is this the time for internal preparation or external action?*

  Life has different seasons and each season can have a different focus. However, each season is a season to dream, even though not every season produces obvious forward movement toward fulfilling your dream. Some seasons involve internal preparation. Others involve rapid and easily observable steps forward. The key is to ask the Father what He is doing in your current season and then partner with His plan for your growth.

  Jesus spent 30 years in preparation for three years of ministry. But not a moment was wasted as He grew in wisdom and understanding and in favor with God and man. Even Jesus needed to grow in favor with God and man! What is the nature of your current season? How can you embrace this season and learn all you need to learn in this time?

- **Timing** – *Is there anything you need to do before proceeding right now?*

  Within each season there is a wide range of potential purpose. You may be in a season of great external growth and opportunity but feel hesitant to move forward on a particular dream. In Mark 1:37-39, we read about Jesus in His season of rapid growth in influence. But just when a revival was breaking out and everyone was open and hungry to hear His message, He moved on to another city. He had a completely different sense of timing than those around Him. His timing was anchored in His relationship with His Father rather than in the recognition of His peers or community.

  You have permission to wait. You have permission to protect your priorities. You have permission to change your course. Is there something you need to do first? Is there a relationship that you need to strengthen before you launch forward? Does your perspective need to embrace a bigger picture or purpose?

THE COST OF A DREAM

Every dream has a cost, a price that must be paid. The bigger your dream is, the greater the cost *and* the greater the reward. Some costs are obvious and up-front. Other costs may be hidden from your current view. You may not fully know all the costs before stepping out, but are you ready to do what is necessary to complete your Dream Journey? How can you keep your eyes on the finish line?

"Aim at Heaven and you will get Earth thrown in. Aim at Earth and you will get neither."

C.S. Lewis

DREAM ACTIVATION EXERCISE: The Cost of a Dream

What is the cost of *not* pursuing your dream? Consider your dream and those who will benefit from it. Look into the eyes of the people your dream will touch. How will their lives be impacted if you *don't* proceed?

....

....

....

....

....

DREAM ACTIVATION EXERCISE: Keeping Passion Alive

Make a plan to stay connected to the passion behind your dream. What is your underlying motivation? How can you keep that passion alive?

Ideas to keep my passion alive:

....

....

....

....

....

....

....

....

....

Dream
JOURNEY

What one thing will I do differently this week to keep the passion for my dream alive?

Dream
JOURNEY

Going Further

No Dream is Accomplished in Isolation

DREAM ACTIVATION EXERCISE (*group*)

Think of one dream you have accomplished. Stand to your feet with this dream in mind. Now, as you are standing, think of the people who helped you at some point on your Dream Journey. Maybe that was someone who invested resources or encouragement into your dream. Maybe that was someone who ran alongside you. Maybe it was a parent, a teacher, a leader or an inspirational figure from history.

If there was anyone who helped you at some point on your Dream Journey, sit down.

Now look around. How many people are still standing? How many people accomplished their dreams entirely on their own? What does that tell you about your need for other people and a supportive community?

....

....

....

BUILDING A CULTURE, A COMMUNITY OF DREAMERS

"For the first time in my life, I feel valuable."

At some point on our Dream Journey we all need help from others. Likewise, we all have something to offer others on their journey. Whether it is encouragement, wisdom, resources or a helping hand, we all have something we can give.

Our dream is to catalyze a Global Dream Culture where each person intentionally seeks to encourage and empower other people in their community to discover their purpose and live out their dreams. In order for this to become a reality, each of us needs to fully embrace our own Dream Journey and then commit to sowing into the dreams of the people around us.

At the core of a Dream Culture beats a heart to see other people live out their dreams. In practice it is about learning to become a better friend. What dreams are waiting to be released in the people around you? What is the passion behind their dreams? What is holding them back from moving forward? And most importantly, how can you help unlock their dreams? How can you pour encouragement into their Dream Journey?

DREAM ACTIVATION EXERCISE: Building Community

Turn to someone next to you. Choose who will go first. Have them share one of their dreams. Ask them to tell you more about that dream. What's the motivation that inspires this dream? What would it look like to fully accomplish this dream? How would that feel?

Once you have heard their dream and explored more about it, swap roles and share one of your dreams. Have them ask you some of the same questions.

What happened when you explored your neighbor's dream? What did you learn about them that you did not know? What surprised you?

....

....

....

....

....

Dream
JOURNEY

"One of the greatest diseases is to be nobody to anybody."

Mother Teresa

WHERE TO FROM HERE?

- **Dream and start acting on those dreams - What is in your hand?**

"Dreams are powerful. Dreams and those who live them can change cultures, redirect nations and move mountains."

Tony Stoltzfus

"Every great dream begins with a dreamer. Always remember, you have within you the strength, the patience, and the passion to reach for the stars to change the world."

Harriet Tubman

Make it a daily habit to follow through on simple decisions and actions that keep moving you toward your dream. You will be amazed how "suddenly" you are living many of your dreams. Consider getting yourself a Dream Journal or starting a blog to record your adventures. Maybe you could even put pictures of your dreams in conspicuous places where you will bump into them often – in the pages of your favorite book or magazine, over the bathroom mirror, on the refrigerator door or even on the dashboard of your car. Release the creativity you were born with, dream bigger and live louder!

There is more of God beyond your fingertips.

- **Find a Dream Friend or Dream Partner**

    Build a relationship with someone who can become a Dream Friend or Dream Partner, someone who will encourage you and help keep you accountable in the pursuit of your dreams. Maybe you could even do this for each other. Look for someone who will love you enough to ask the hard questions. Find a friend who will not allow their

own disappointments, fears or limitations to spill out on you and quench your dreams, but will instead pour more fuel on your fire. Both of you need to hear encouraging comments and questions from each other like these:

"Wow! That dream is amazing!"

"How are you getting on with your dreams?"

"What steps have you made this week to move toward those dreams becoming reality?"

"What is stopping you from moving forward on that dream?"

"When was the last time you sat down to dream again and dream even bigger!"

- **Encourage the dreams of the people around you**

  Freely you have received, now freely give. You have a testimony that can unlock dreams in the lives of other people. Just being around somebody who is experiencing life more abundantly is a contagious experience. People everywhere are just waiting for someone to believe in them. You have what it takes. Every day we literally bump into people who need encouragement as much as a baby needs food. Without encouragement life becomes stunted and drained of energy and fun. Who will you bump into today, intentionally or not? Who could you encourage today in their Dream Journey? It is amazing how even a smile can encourage someone's day.

- **Develop a toolbox of questions**

  Develop your toolbox of both questioning skills and attentive listening skills. But even more importantly, listen to the One who asks the most powerful questions—the Holy Spirit.

  "I believe in you! What is your dream?"

  "What five things can you do now to start moving toward that dream?"

  "What will you do?"

  "When do you plan on completing that?"

  "What do you already have in your hand that you can use to start?"

  "How can I help keep you on track?"

Our purpose for creating these Dream Journey tools goes above and beyond any desire to bring you just another book or program. Our dream is that together we will create

a culture where each one of us intentionally looks for ways to help one another bring our dreams into reality.

You now hold the baton... **What will you do with it?**

*The world is waiting to see what picture your life paints
of who He is, so live well!*

If you would like further information, please contact us at **www.iDreamCulture.com.**

We would love to hear testimonies of dreams coming true and dreamers being inspired and empowered on their Dream Journey.

Thanks for partnering with us to catalyze hope and develop a Global Dream Culture, a culture on earth "...as it is in Heaven."

Grace on your Dream Journey!

Dream JOURNEY

Resources to help you on your Dream Journey

One way to unlock more dreams is to write down at least one dream for each question below. If you are a natural dreamer, that is you easily envision the future even when you don't know how to get there, use the first set of questions. If you are a more matter-of-fact person and have a hard time detaching yourself from "what is" to think about what "could be," try the second list.

Dream Starters for Natural Dreamers

- What gives you pleasure?

- What is beautiful for you?

- What do you want to do just for fun?

- If you were fearless, what would you try?

- What do you value most in the world?

- What do you need?

- What needs of others tug at your heart?

- Who do you dream for, and what is your dream for them?

101

- If you could change one thing in the world, what would it be?

- What would Heaven on Earth look like to you?

- What do you dream will happen when you get to Heaven?

- Who do you know who is living their dream? What do you love about their life?

- What thought or idea have you had that you haven't acted on—maybe you thought it was too big, too foolish or too inconsequential to identify as a dream?

- What would make your spiritual life really soar? Your emotional life? Your physical life?

- What would you do if money were no limitation?

Dream Starters for Others

- What in your life gives you pleasure now? Which of those things could you do more of now?

- Where have you seen beauty in life? Which of these things would you like to have more of in your life now?

- What do you do for fun, when you really cut loose or aren't worried so much about what it costs?

- What is the most fearless thing you have done? What else would you try if you felt like that?

- What do you value most in the world? How could that increase?

- What do you need? What would it look like if that need were filled? What needs of others tug at your heart?

- Who do you know that you want to help have a better life? What would you do for them if you could?

- If you could change one thing in the world, what would it be?

- Where have you most clearly seen Heaven on earth? Would you like to see more of that?

- What do you dream will happen to you when you get to Heaven?

- Who do you know that is living their dream? What do you love about their life?

- What thought or idea have you had that you haven't acted on; maybe you thought it was too big or too foolish or too inconsequential to qualify as a valid dream?

- What makes your spiritual life really soar? Your emotional life? Your physical life?

More Dream Starters

What thoughts and dreams do the following examples trigger in you?

- **Professional dreams** - Be the top salesperson for the year. Gain national accreditation.

- **Family dreams** - Get married. Be the best father I can be.

- **Financial dreams** - Pay off all credit card debt. Grow five sources of income.

- **Creative dreams** - Paint a mural in a public place. Write a song for my children.

- **Places to visit** - The Great Wall of China; the place where my grandparents were born.

- **Skills to master** - Gourmet BBQ chef; golf handicap less than 10.

- **Books to read** - The Bible from cover to cover; one book every month.

- **Events to attend** - A U2 concert; 4th of July in New York.

- **Subjects to research** - The history of America, divine health.

- **Things you've always wanted to do** - Bungee jump; sleep the night in a mud hut.

- **Subjects you want to study** - Gravity, history, Spanish.

- **Places you want to visit** - The Great Pyramids; Dunkirk; New Zealand.

- **Experiences you want to have** - Hot air balloon ride; scuba diving off the Great Barrier Reef.

- **Food you want to eat** - Seven-course meal; Medieval birthday party.

- **People you want to meet** - Bono; Mohammad Yunus, The President.

- **Countries you want to visit** - Russia; Turkey; Tahiti; Israel; the "newest" and "oldest."

- **Hobbies you want to have** - Model plane building; cake decorating; golf.

- **Kind of partner you want to have** - Lover of Jesus; creative; wise.

- **Children and grandchildren you want to have** - Smarter than me; go further and faster.

- **Things you want to have** - An income while I sleep; a house; a yellow Chevy Camaro with black stripes.

- **Things you want to buy** - A digital camera; a world-trip for my wife; a house.

- **Sports you want to try** - American football; lacrosse; cross-country skiing.

- **Physical condition you want to be in** - Less than 200 pounds; able to run five miles at any time.

- **How you would like to look** - Sharp and confidant, but relaxed and friendly.

- **Feelings you want to feel** - Euphoria of conquering a mountain; overwhelmed by love.

- **Gifts you want to give** - A house to a pastor in Africa; a million dollars at one time.

- **The kind of lifestyle you want to have** - 30 hours a week "working" and more time with children.

- **The friends you want to have** - A president; a homeless man; a Muslim cleric.

- **The way you want to spend time with friends** - Adventures outdoors; living their dreams.

- **The relationship you want to have with your family** - Powerful, free and happy.

- **The financial freedom you want to be in** - Leave an inheritance for my children's children.

- **The toys you would want to buy yourself** – Remote Control off-road car; model railway; crossbow.

- **The charity you want to contribute to** - My own; World Vision; Opportunity International.

- **The thing you want to be remembered for** - Love; empowering others; miracles.

Recommended Reading

A Leader's Life Purpose Workbook by Tony Stoltzfus. www.coach22.com, 2009.

Coaching Questions by Tony Stoltzfus. www.coach22.com, 2008.

Cracks in the Foundation by Steve Backlund. www.ignitedhope.com, 2007.

Dream Manager by Matthew Kelly. Beacon Publishing, 2007.

Face to Face With God by Bill Johnson. Destiny Image, 2007.

Put Your Dream to the Test by John C. Maxwell. Thomas Nelson, 2009.

Strengthen Yourself in the Lord by Bill Johnson. Destiny Image, 2007.

The Seven Habits of Highly Effective People by Stephen R. Covey, 2004.

The Dream Giver by Bruce Wilkinson. Multnomah Publishers, 2003.

Victorious Mindsets by Steve Backlund. www.ignitedhope.com, 2008.

References

Collins Concise English Dictionary. New Zealand Edition Edited by Ian A. Gordon. 1982. William Collins Sons & Co Ltd.

Coaching Questions: A Coach's Guide to Powerful Asking Skills
by Tony Stoltzfus. 2008. www.coach22.com.

Dream Culture: Bringing Dreams To Life
by Andy & Janine Mason. 2011. http://www.idreamculture.com.

Leadership Coaching: The Disciplines, Skills and Heart of a Christian Coach
by Tony Stoltzfus. 2005. www.coach22.com.

Merriam-Webster.com. 2011. http://www.merriam-webster.com (8 May 2011).

About the Authors...

Andy and Janine Mason come from the beautiful east coast of New Zealand. Together with their four elementary aged children and ten suitcases, they arrived in Redding, California in August of 2008. They had a dream to give their lives to develop people. Little did they know that they would soon be partnering with Danny Silk and his new team at Bethel Church helping build an organization to build the lives of people.

Andy and Janine are now directors of *Dream Culture* and part of the leadership team for Global Transformation Institute. Started in early 2010, *Dream Culture* is a ministry that encourages and empowers people to discover their dreams and make practical steps to live out their purpose. What began at Bethel Church is now catalyzing dreamers and Dream Cultures in schools, businesses, churches and community groups around the world.

Before coming to Redding, Andy worked for a leading financial institution and a national consultancy firm. His primary role was in helping clients define what success was to them, then partnering with them in developing strategic plans towards realizing that success. Andy was also involved for ten years in the leadership team of a local church in New Zealand.

Janine's background is in people development, adult training and project management, for both non-profit and profit-based organizations. In addition to being a wonderful mother to four children, Janine is known for her perceptive questions that quickly help clients get to the heart of the matter and develop practical and holistic approaches for moving forward.

In January 2011, Janine and Andy published their first book, *Dream Culture: Bringing Dreams to Life* (also available in Spanish).

For more information please visit:
www.idreamculture.com